GW01144616

Discover the Heart of God

Pamela Gough Bahash
Illustrated by January Jorgenson

Evergreen
PRESS

Dedication

This book is dedicated to my late husband,
Peter Gough, and my oldest son,
Justin Gough, who are rejoicing together
in the presence of Almighty God.
They have discovered him face to face
in a way that you and I can only imagine.
—*Pamela Gough Bahash*

To my parents, Wendell and Arlyne
—*January Jorgenson*

Discover the Heart of God by Pamela Gough Bahash
Copyright ©2005 Pamela Gough Bahash
All rights reserved. This book is protected under the copyright laws of the United States of America. This book may not be copied or reprinted for commercial gain or profit. Unless otherwise identified, Scripture quotations are taken from *The Holy Bible, New King James Version*, Copyright © 1979, 1980, 1982 by Thomas Nelson, Inc. Those marked NAS are taken from the *New American Standard Bible*, ©The Lockman Foundation, 1960, 1962, 1963, 1971, 1972, 1973, 1974. Those marked NIV are taken from *The Holy Bible, New International Version*, copyright © 1978 by New York International Bible Society. All rights reserved. Used by permission.

ISBN 1-58169-198-X
Printed in Korea • For Worldwide Distribution

Evergreen Press, P.O. Box 191540, Mobile, AL 36619

A Gift For...

Molly

From

Ruth McAllister

1 - 8 - 2013

(Dundrum)

Preface

Can we know who God is and what He is like? In the Bible, God describes Himself by revealing His attributes that explain His nature and His character. He is a real person with emotions and values, and He is calling to you:

For I know the thoughts that I have toward you, says the Lord, thoughts of peace and not of evil, to give you a future and a hope. Then you will call upon Me and go and pray to Me and I will listen to you. And you will seek Me and find Me, when you search for Me with all your heart (Jeremiah 29:11-13).

Getting to know God is something we do with our hearts. So open your heart to God and begin to explore His heart. As you discover His personality, you will want to talk with Him in prayer. Read the sample prayer on each page, and then offer your own thoughts to Him.

—*Pamela Gough Bahash*

Table of Contents

God is…My Creator 7
God is…Unchanging 11
God is…Full of Glory 15
God is…Love 19
God is…Eternal 23
God is…Omnipresent 27
God is…Righteous 31
God is…Just 35
God is…Good 39
God is…Patient 43
God is…My Protector 47
God is…My Provider 51
God is…My Guide 55
God is…Faithful 59

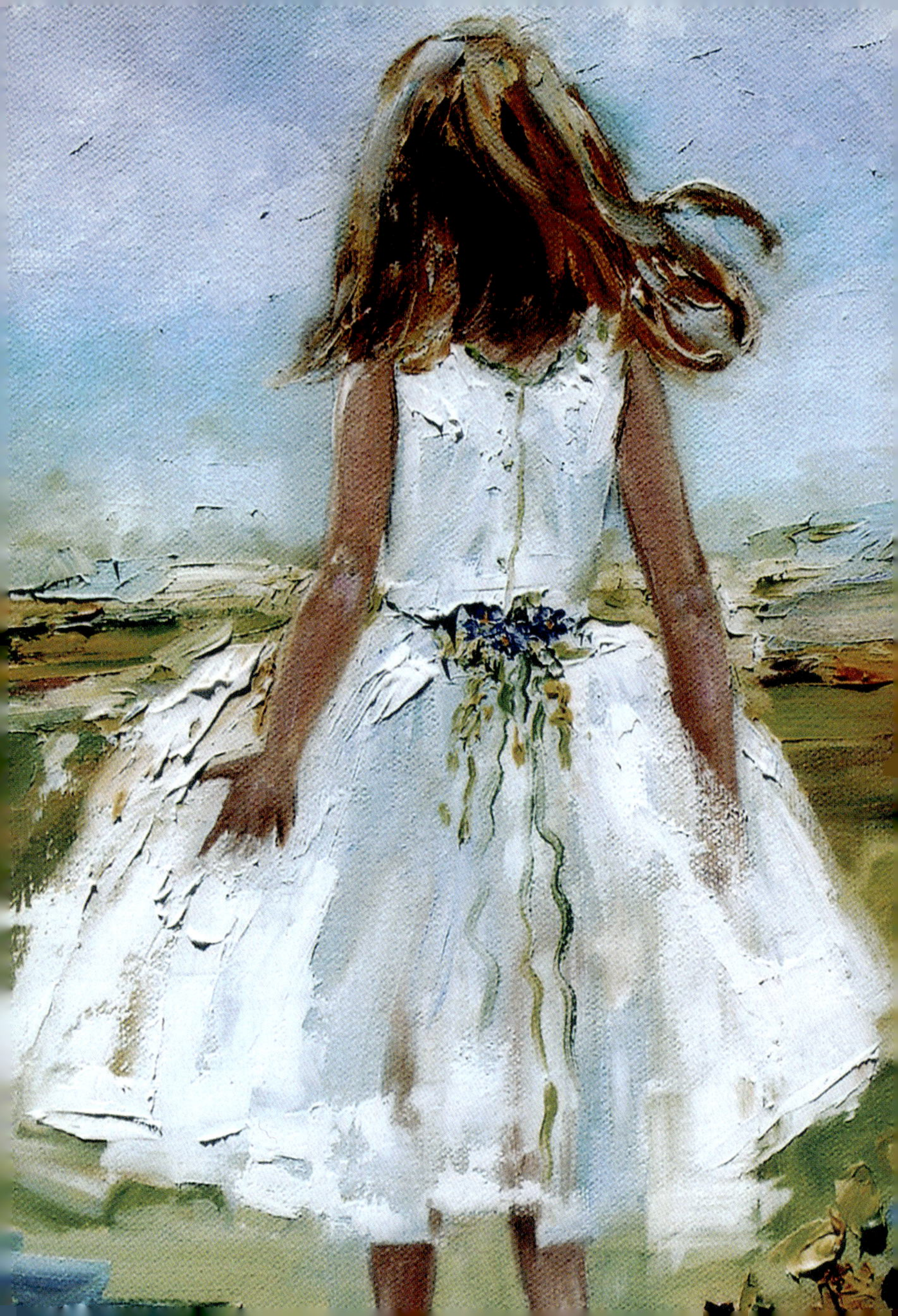

God Is...
MY CREATOR

The Bible opens with these words, "In the beginning God created the heavens and the earth." We cannot see God, but we can learn a lot about what He is like from His creation. One thing that is obvious is that He must love you and me very much. When He created the world for us, He was like a parent preparing the nursery for a new baby, desiring to fill it with things that would stimulate all of our senses.

He made beautiful things for our eyes to see and amazing sounds for us to hear, including music! He gave us wonderful things to taste and smell, and the desire to touch and be touched. When we consider just one thing – flowers – how amazing it is to see all the varieties and kinds of flowers; all the colors and fragrances! Surely flowers are a gift from His heart to ours. How awesome God must be. And as we look around us, how can we not long to meet our Creator and be willing to search for Him with all our hearts!

Faithful Father...

Your creation tells me that you are very special. I want to know you better. Help me to draw closer to you...please come into my life and make yourself real to me. AMEN.

Words to Live By

"Let the heavens rejoice, and let the earth be glad; Let the sea roar, and all its fullness; Let the field be joyful, and all that is in it."

"Then the trees of the woods will rejoice before the Lord.... Let the rivers clap their hands; Let the hills be joyful together before the Lord...."

"Know that the Lord, He is God; It is He who has made us, and not we ourselves; We are His people and the sheep of His pasture.... Be thankful to Him, and bless His name."
Psalm 96:11 & 12; 98:8; 100:3 & 4

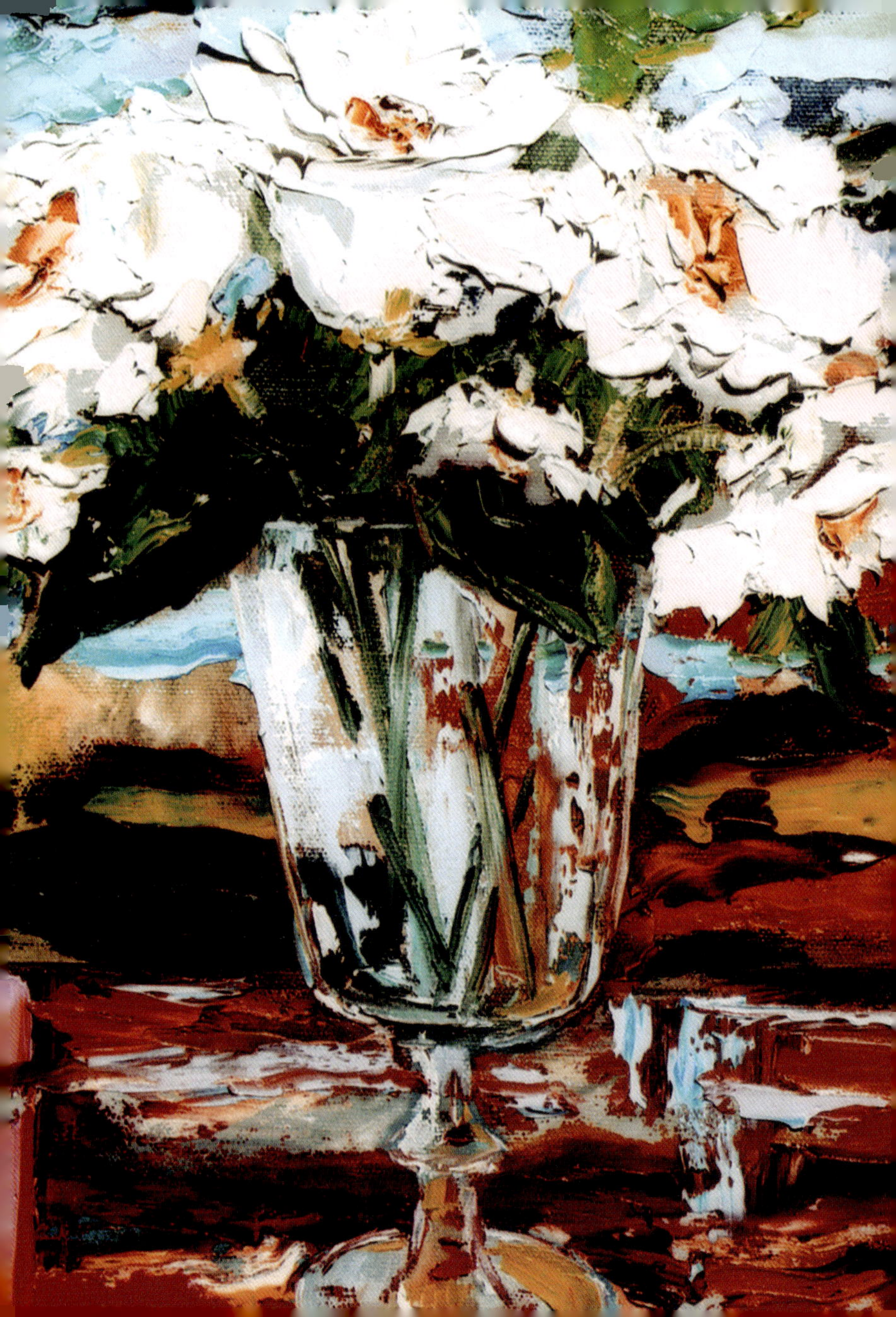

God Is...
UNCHANGING

We sometimes use flowers to say "I'm sorry" when we hurt the people we love. Human nature is such that our feelings are constantly changing. And we often treat others based on how we are feeling.

God's unchanging nature sets Him apart from everyone else. He does not change his mind. His purpose is fixed, and His word is sure. He will always reward good and correct evil. The Bible compares God to a rock that cannot be moved. And the feelings God has towards us will never change. He is not influenced by our behavior. There is nothing we can do to make God love us more, and even when we sin, He will not love us less. He loves us with an everlasting love.

Heavenly Father...

It seems that things never stay the same for long. My feelings are up and down and I am always living on the edge, not knowing what tomorrow will hold for me. Help me to remember to call out to you. I know I can put my trust in you in a world that is constantly changing. Please be my rock. AMEN.

Words to Live By

"The Lord is near to all who call upon Him...He will hear their cry and save them...The Lord preserves all who love Him...." Psalms 145:18-20

"I am the Lord, I change not." Malachi 3:6

"It is impossible for God to lie...." Hebrews 6:18

"God is not a man, that He should lie, nor a son of man, that He should change his mind...." Numbers 23:19 NIV

"The Lord is my rock and my fortress and my deliverer...." Psalms 18:2

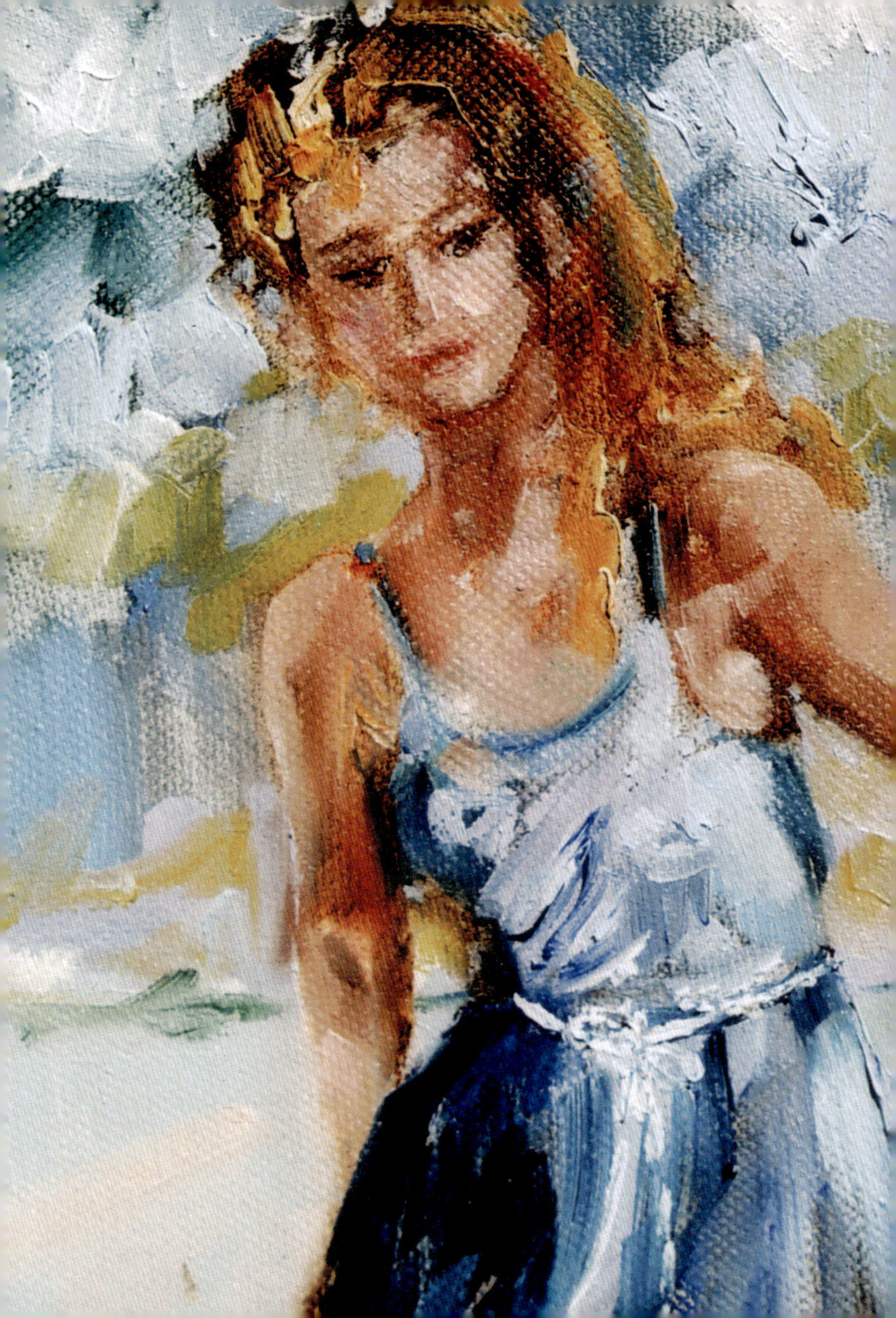

God Is...
FULL OF GLORY

The prophet Isaiah heard the angels in heaven declare that "the whole earth is full of God's glory." What did they mean by that? How can we, here on the earth, see the glory of God?

The fact is that we are surrounded by God's glory...it is everywhere! When we look into the sky we see His glory in the sun, the moon and the stars. When we walk through a meadow, or hike up a mountain, or visit the ocean, we are brought face to face with the glory of God. He is never far from us. We can feel His presence in a powerful way through His many works. One day we will see God in His glory.

As God's children, we can also give glory to God. We make choices everyday that show God respect or disrespect. As you and I take opportunities to honor Him with our lips or with our lives, God feels the pride of a parent watching his child achieve great things.... His heart bursts with excitement as He sees us mature and grow in attitude and character. When we reflect His heart, He is glorified.

Glorious Lord...

Help me to slow down enough each day to catch a glimpse of your glory revealed all around me in your creation. Sometimes I use your name in a way that does not show you respect. Please forgive me. I want to glorify you with my thoughts, my words, and my whole life. AMEN.

Words to Live By

"The heavens declare the glory of God; the skies proclaim the work of His hands." Psalm 19:1

"O Lord, how manifold are Your works! In wisdom you have made them all. The earth is full of your possessions.... This great and wide sea, in which are innumerable teeming things, living things both small and great.... These all wait for You, that You may give them their food in due season.... May the glory of the Lord endure forever; I will sing to the Lord as long as I live; Bless the Lord, O my soul! Praise the Lord!"
Psalm 104: excerpts from v. 24-35

"...glorify God in your body and in your spirit, which are God's." 1 Corinthians 6:20

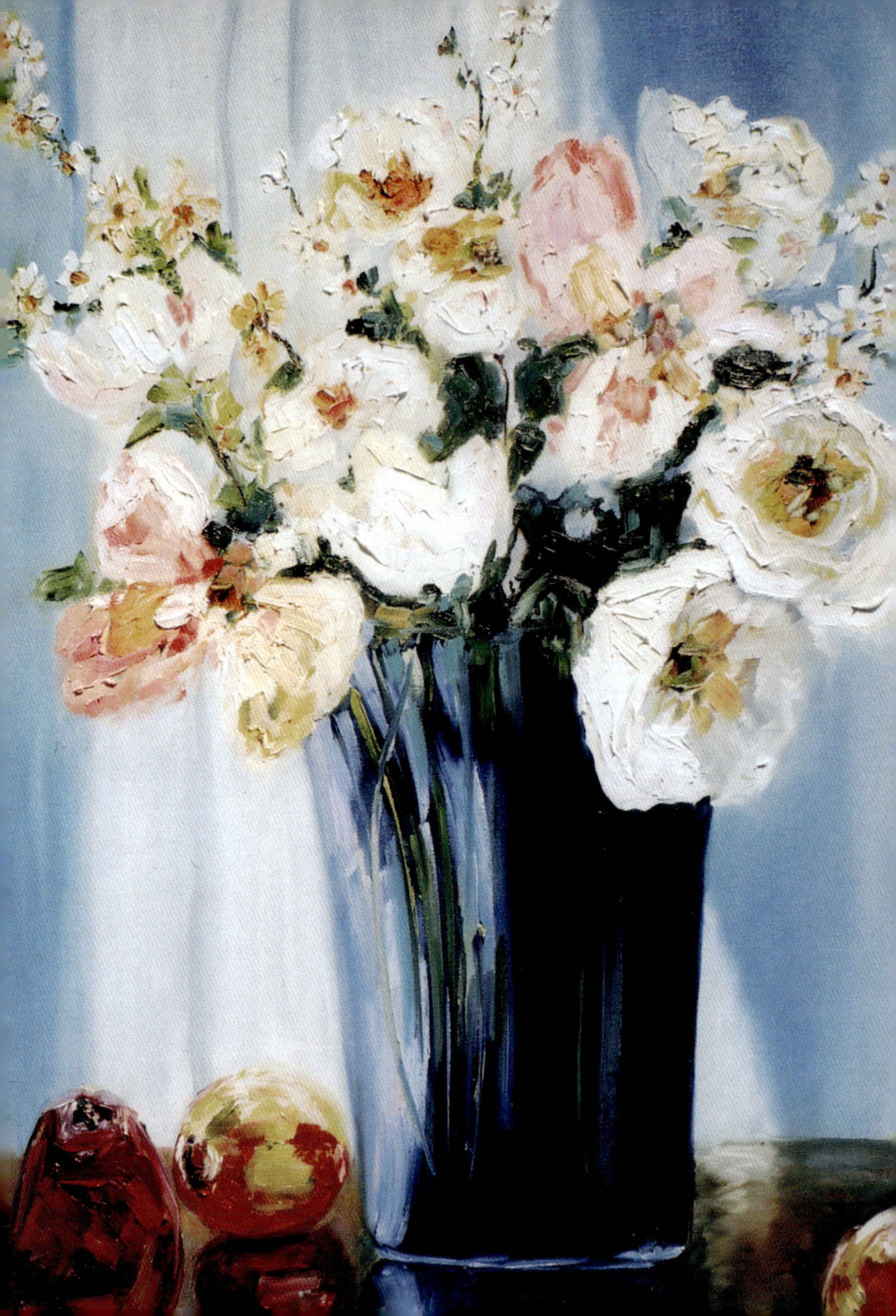

God Is...
LOVE

God doesn't "feel" love; but rather He "is" love. His love for us is based on who He is, and not on anything we do.

The Bible is a love story. It is the true account of His great love and desire to bring about His divine purpose for each one of us. It opens with creation and the disobedience of the first humans. They hid from God because they were afraid. In His tender mercy, He went and found them. He did not destroy them and start over, because He loved them and already loved all of their descendents, including us! Instead, He provided a Redeemer. In the person of Jesus Christ we have a way of forgiveness and access to God. The Bible closes with this final appeal from Jesus, "Come and drink life's water free."

Have you responded to God's love? Jesus advised you and I to "Love the Lord your God with all your heart, with all your soul, and with all your mind." And, "love your neighbor as yourself."

Just imagine what the world would be like if everyone did that!

Loving Father...

The Bible says you know how many hairs are on my head and you see every little bird that falls. How could I ever doubt your love for me? The sad thing is sometimes I do. Please forgive me for not trusting you. Help me to find ways to express my faith, and to show love to others. AMEN.

Words to Live By

"Before I formed you in the womb I knew you…" Jeremiah 1:5

"…God is love. In this the love of God was manifested toward us, that God has sent His only begotten Son into the world, that we might live through Him. We love Him because He first loved us." 1 John 4:8-9 & 19

"…Yes, I have loved you with an everlasting love; Therefore with lovingkindness I have drawn you." Jeremiah 31:3

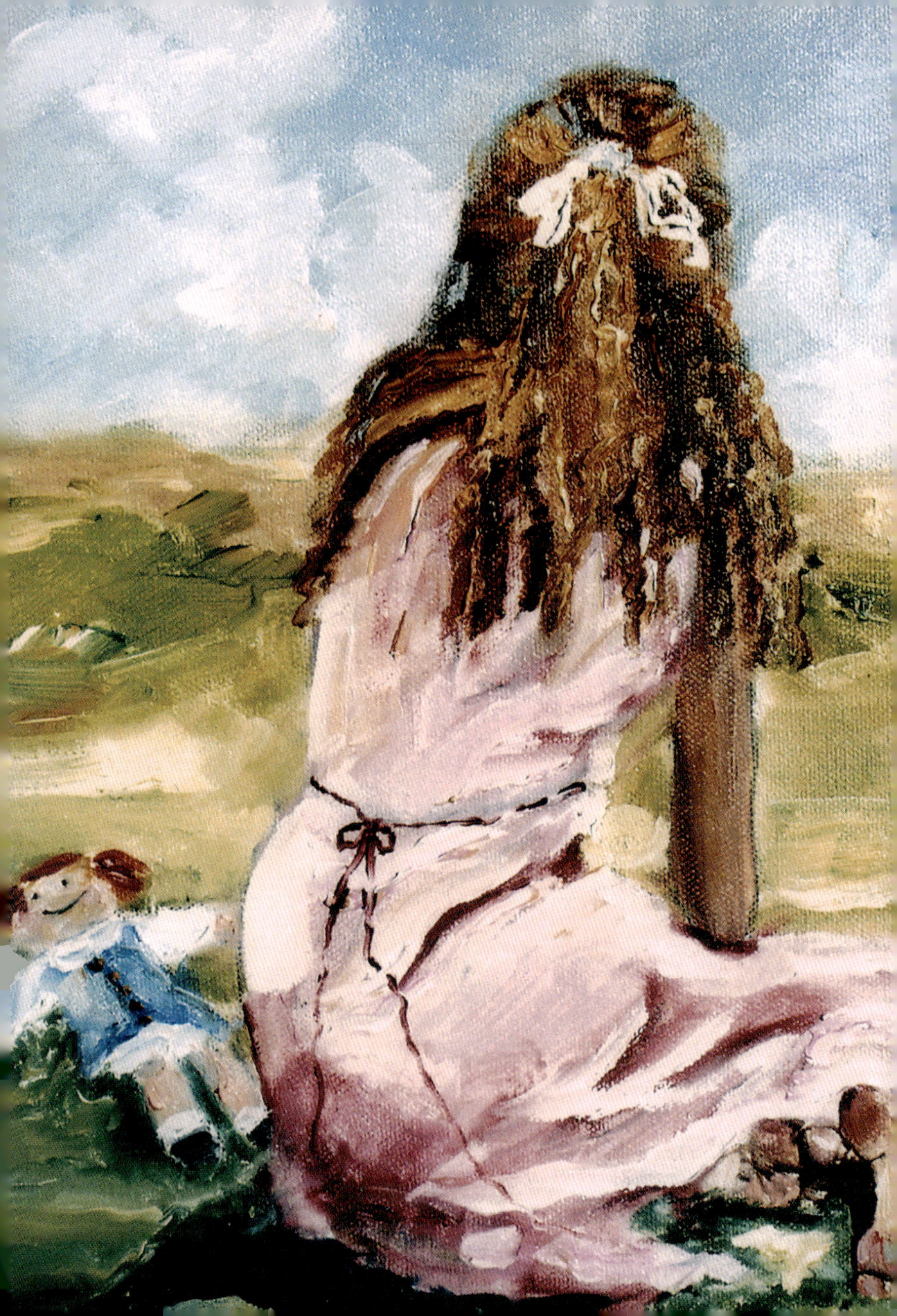

God Is...
ETERNAL

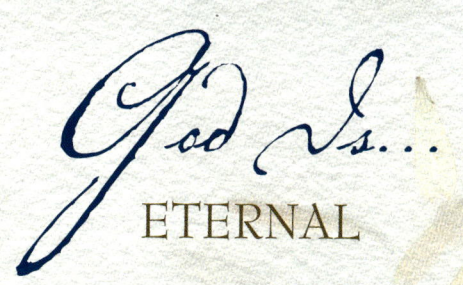

Children are content to live in the moment! In the midst of playing, they forget everything else. They happily take one day at a time and don't worry about the future. As adults, our lives are more complicated. Our days are filled with activity, but we seldom feel content. How can we learn to be at peace in a frantic world?

God is eternal, existing forever; and He has promised eternal life to those who trust in Him. But eternal life is not just for the future. It is the promise of an abundant, full life today. When we trust in God, you and I begin a new adventure as He helps us to take the path that He has prepared for us.

And because we will live eternally, we can focus on what is really important...things that will be around forever – people rather than possessions, character rather than popularity, and righteousness rather than temporary gratification. As we read the Word of God and learn His ways, we will develop an eternal perspective on our life.

Heavenly Father...

I can't follow someone that I am running ahead of! Sometimes I go chasing after my own hopes and dreams without slowing down enough to let you guide me. Please help me to learn to wait on you. Give me the desire to spend more time in your Word, so I can understand your heart. The better I know you, the more content I will be with myself. AMEN.

Words to Live By

"Be still, and know that I am God…" Psalm 46:10

"For the wages of sin is death, but the gift of God is eternal life in Christ Jesus our Lord." Romans 6:23

"…Eye has not seen, nor ear heard, nor have entered into the heart of man the things which God has prepared for those who love Him."
1 Corinthians 2:13

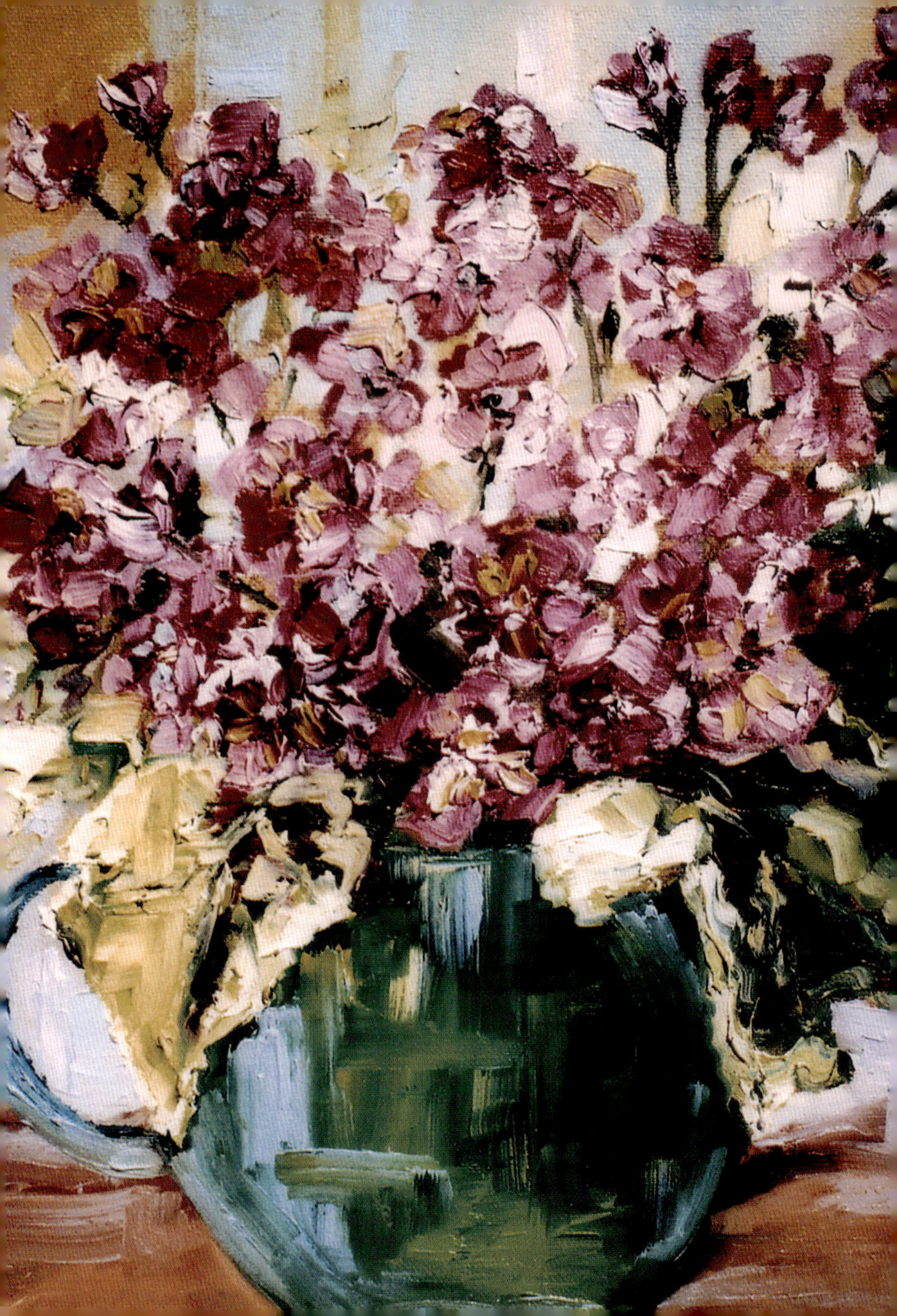

God Is...
OMNIPRESENT

Because we cannot see God with our eyes, some foolishly have concluded that He does not exist. We cannot see or touch air, but if it was removed, we would know it immediately! Every human being consists of a body, soul and spirit; and it is by our spirit that we perceive God and sense His presence. The Bible tells us that God is omnipresent – He is everywhere all the time. When we pray, even though thousands of people are also praying at the same time, He can hear every word we say!

In order to find God, you and I must approach Him through our hearts. God says we will find Him if we seek Him with all our "heart." God is so close to each of us, that He knows what we are thinking and the desires of our heart. He is the only one that can meet our deep longings; and if we can enter into His presence, we will experience the peace and fulfillment that only He can give.

Loving Lord...

Forgive me for feeling alone when I know that you are so close to me that you know what I am thinking and feeling all the time. Please help me to be more aware of your presence. I am guilty of looking to other people and things in this world to satisfy my empty heart, but I know true contentment comes from feeling close to you. That is what I desire more than anything. AMEN.

Words to Live By

"The fool has said in his heart, 'There is no God.' God looks down from heaven upon the children of men, to see if there are any who understand, who seek God." Psalm 53:1 & 2

"'Am I a God near at hand' says the Lord, 'and not a God afar off? Can anyone hide himself in secret places, so I shall not see him?' says the Lord. 'Do I not fill heaven and earth?' says the Lord." Jeremiah 23:23 & 24

"…In your presence is fullness of joy; at your right hand are pleasures forevermore." Psalm 16:11

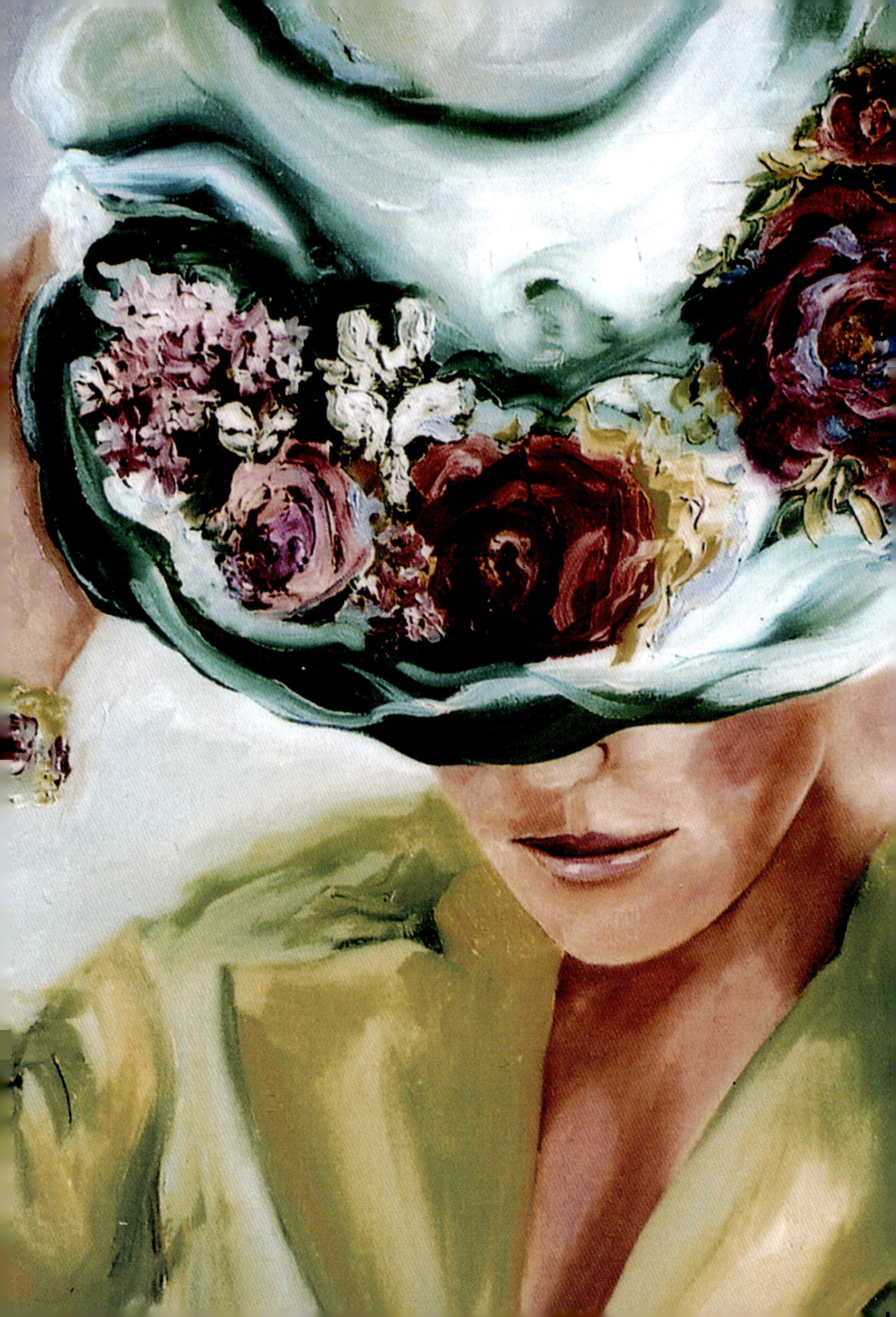

God Is...
RIGHTEOUS

Righteous is not a word we hear much anymore. Simply put, it means "right thinking" and "right living." God is righteous in all His ways. He never has impure motives, and His actions always perfectly conform to His other attributes, such as love, goodness and justice.

In simpler times, right thinking and right living were more clearly defined. Today, because there are so many lifestyles offered and ethical choices for you and I to make, sometimes we struggle to know what is right!

The fact is that without God's help, none of us can be righteous. The Bible tells us that when we put our trust in the Lord Jesus Christ, God gives us a renewed heart — one that desires to live righteously. And the Holy Spirit helps us to do it. Without Christ, any righteousness that we have is simply "self-righteousness." The Lord promises that if we choose to pursue His righteousness He will give us everything else we need, including true fulfillment and joy that can only come from obedience to Him.

Faithful Father...

I am so tired of trying to be righteous in my own strength. I constantly fail, and many times when I do something good, it is for the wrong motives. Please cleanse my heart of any self righteousness. Create in me new attitudes and character goals and fill me with your Holy Spirit, so that I am able to carry them out in your power and strength. Teach me to think rightly and live rightly. I want to experience true joy and contentment. AMEN.

Words to Live By

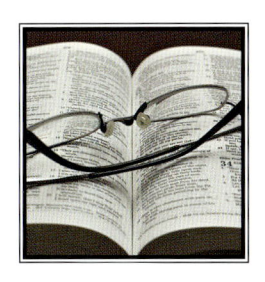

"Create in me a clean heart, O God, and renew a steadfast spirit within me." Psalm 51:10

"Therefore, if anyone is in Christ, he is a new creation; old things have passed away; behold all things have become new.... For He made Him who knew no sin to be sin for us, that we might become the righteousness of God in Him."
2 Corinthians 5:17 & 21

"Therefore do not worry, saying "What shall we eat?" "What shall we drink?" or "What shall we wear?" For your heavenly Father knows you need all these things. But seek first the kingdom of God and His righteousness, and all these things shall be added to you." Matthew 6:31 & 33

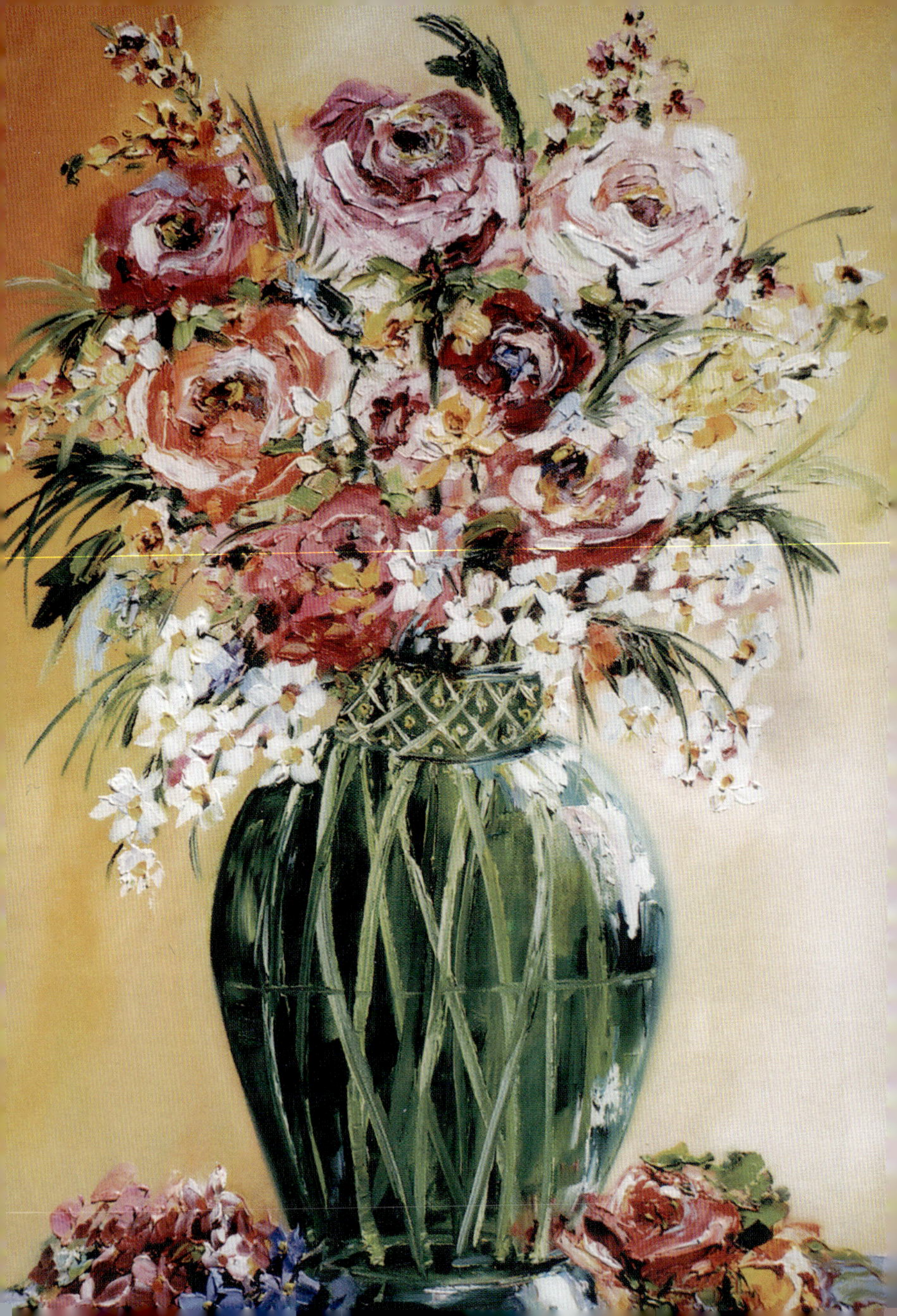

God Is...

JUST

When we read the morning newspaper, we sometimes find ourselves shaking our heads and thinking, "If there is a God, why doesn't He do something!"

The Bible tells us that God does care. He has a plan to deal with evil and injustice. Every time we pray the Lords prayer, "...Thy kingdom come, thy will be done on earth as it is in heaven," we are praying for God's justice.

God desires to make things right with all His children...with you and with me. We can make peace with God today by exercising faith in Jesus Christ. Peace with God means that our fear and dread of the future will be gone! No matter what circumstances we find ourselves in, or what is happening in the world around us, we will have hope and the security that only trusting God can bring.

Gracious Father...

There are so many people hurting because of injustice in the world, and sometimes it's hard for me to understand why you permit it to go on. I long to see an end to violence and tragedy. Thank you for the peace of mind you give me when I trust you. Please guide me to treat others fairly, and help me to forgive those who treat me unjustly. AMEN.

Words to Live By

"The eyes of the Lord are in every place, keeping watch on the evil and the good." Proverbs 15:3

"Lord, how long will the wicked triumph? They utter speech, and speak insolent things; all the workers of iniquity boast in themselves."
Psalm 94:3 & 4

"Therefore, having been justified by faith, we have peace with God through our Lord Jesus Christ."
Romans 5:1

"Let the peace of God rule in your hearts...."
Colossians 3:15

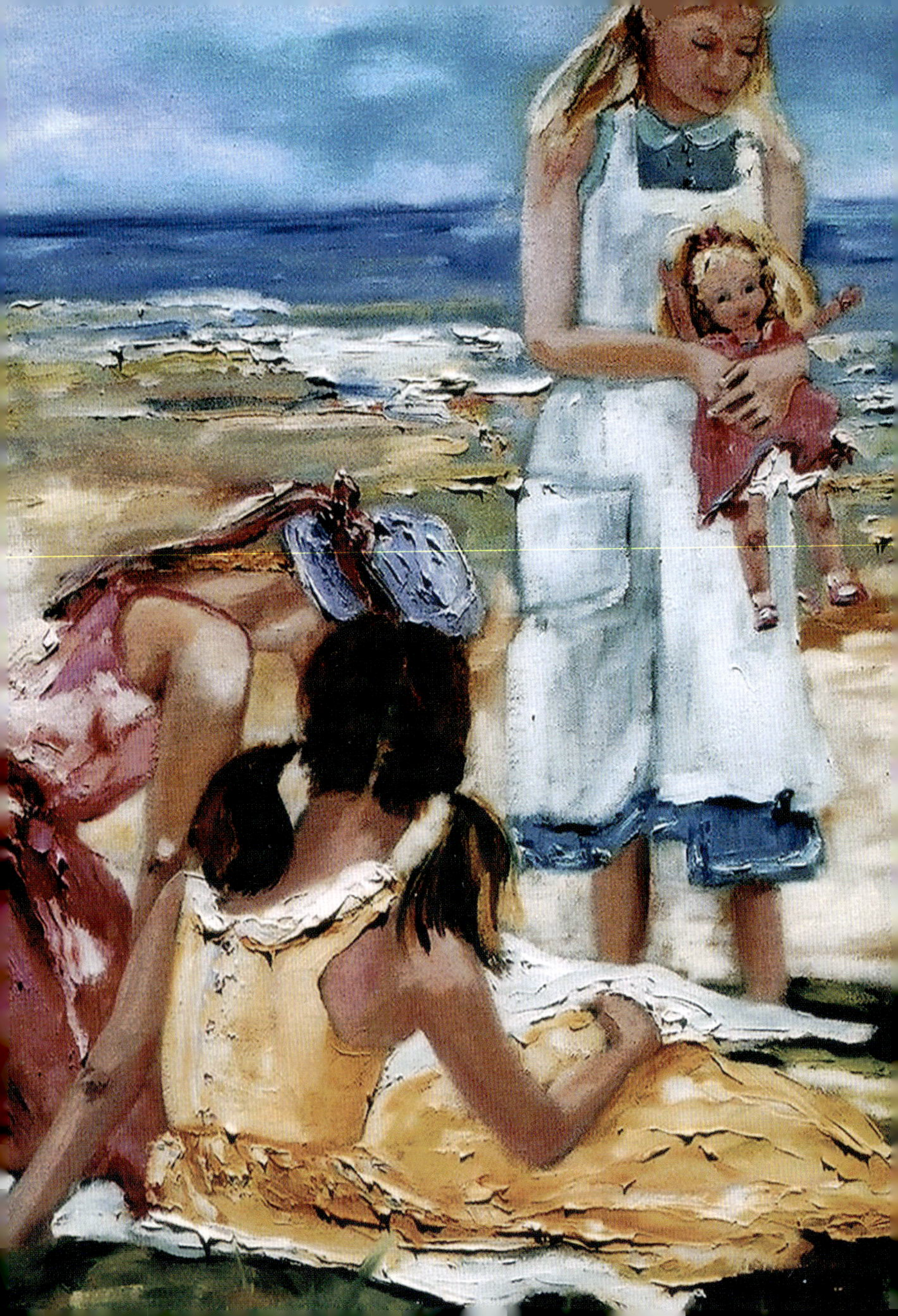

God Is...
GOOD

God is not only the greatest of all living beings, but He is the best. Any goodness in us comes directly from Him. He is the source of all that is good in the universe and everything He does is good. In Genesis 1 He proclaimed each aspect of His creation as "good" and then summed it all up in verse 31 as being "very good"!

So the goodness of God is seen first in creation, and we experience His goodness through what He has made. He fills our lives with pleasures and wonders. A simple visit to the beach can feed our spirit as we feel the hot sand under our feet, breathe in the sea air and watch the waves crash on the shore. This is just a sample of His "tender mercies" in our behalf.

You and I need to take time to meditate on the goodness of God. Just thinking about His goodness to us lifts us out of our mundane daily grind and satisfies our soul in a way that nothing else this side of heaven can do. Start by counting your blessings and naming them one by one!

Merciful Father...

You have given me so many good gifts. Please forgive me for not appreciating your goodness. Thank you for the many blessings that go unnoticed by me each day...the warmth of the sun, the sound of laughter from those I love, and even the little dog that greets me with so much joy. Most of all, thank you that I can know and believe in Jesus Christ. AMEN.

Words to Live By

"The Lord is good to all, and His tender mercies are over all His works." Psalm 145:9

"You are good and do good. Teach me your statutes…I will keep your precepts with my whole heart." Psalm 119:68 & 69

"If you then, being evil, know how to give good gifts to your children, how much more will your Father who is in heaven give good things to those who ask Him!" Matthew 7:11

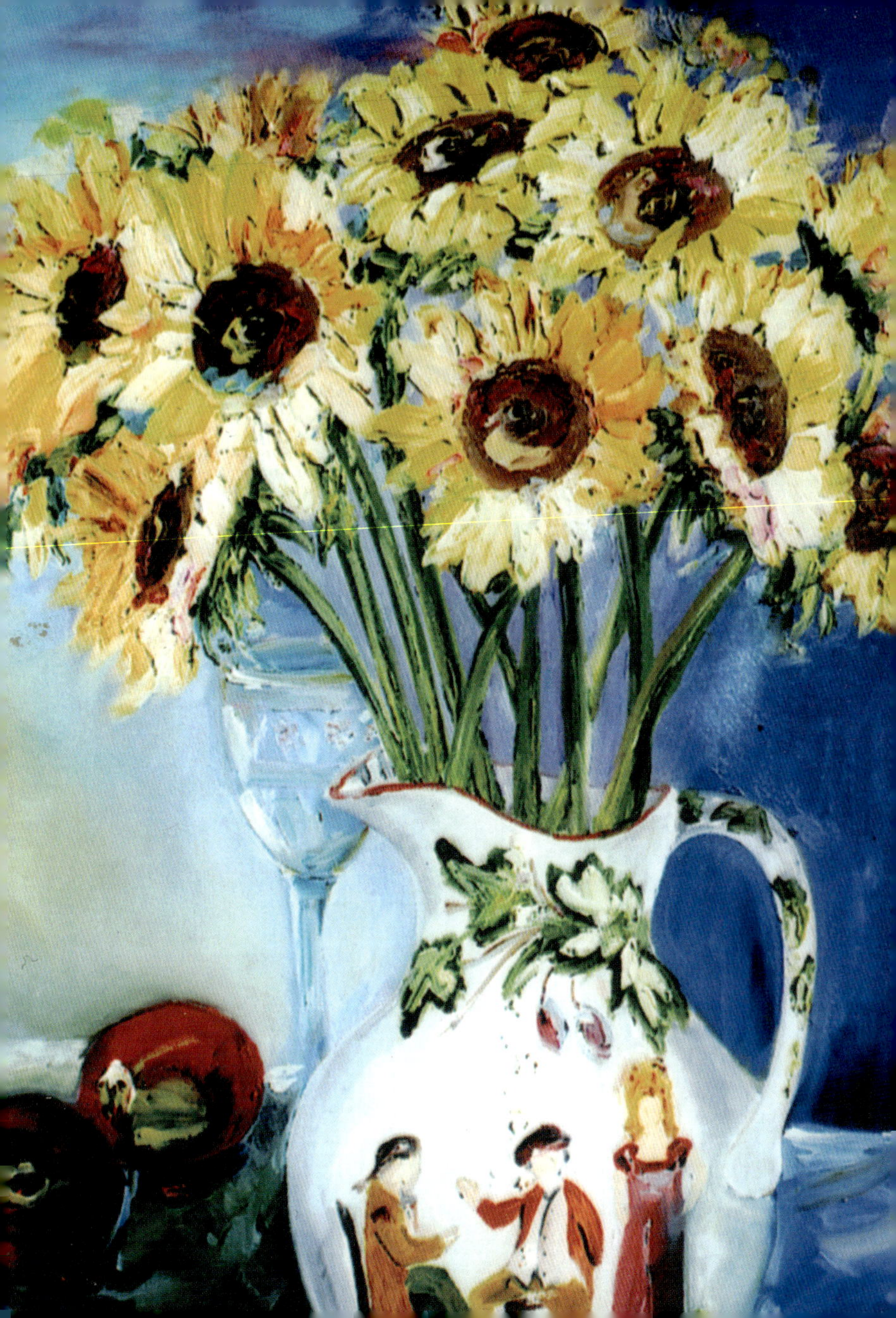

God Is...
PATIENT

Is there someone in your life that tests your patience? Being patient always requires effort, and sometimes it requires a willingness to surrender our personal rights.

In the Bible, God's patience is often called longsuffering. God has the absolute right to remove evil from the world at any time. And yet, He has chosen to exercise patience, or longsuffering, for what seems to us like a very long time.

We get an amazing glimpse into the heart of God here. God's attributes of perfect holiness and justice are balanced by His love and mercy. God loves us so much that He chooses to patiently wait for you and me to respond to His love. He would rather "suffer long" Himself, than have any of His children miss an opportunity to come to know him.

God has chosen to temper justice with mercy. So when we choose to display patience when wronged, we are reflecting God's character. What a privilege you and I have to demonstrate the heart of God!

Gracious Lord...

How amazing you are that you have chosen to be longsuffering for my benefit. Thank you for being patient with me. Forgive me for my constant frustration over every little thing that goes wrong. Please help me to be patient with those that irritate me, and help me to resist demanding my rights in every situation. AMEN.

Words to Live By

"The Lord is not slow about His promise, as some count slowness, but is patient toward you, not wishing for any to perish but for all to come to repentance...therefore, regard the patience of our Lord to be salvation...." 2 Peter 3:7,9 & 15 NAS

"For I say to you, love your enemies, bless those who curse you, do good to those who hate you, and pray for those who spitefully use you and persecute you, that you may be sons of your Father in heaven; for He makes His sun rise on the evil and on the good, and sends rain on the just and on the unjust." Matthew 5:44 & 45

"Now may the God of patience and comfort grant you to be like-minded toward one another...." Romans 15:6

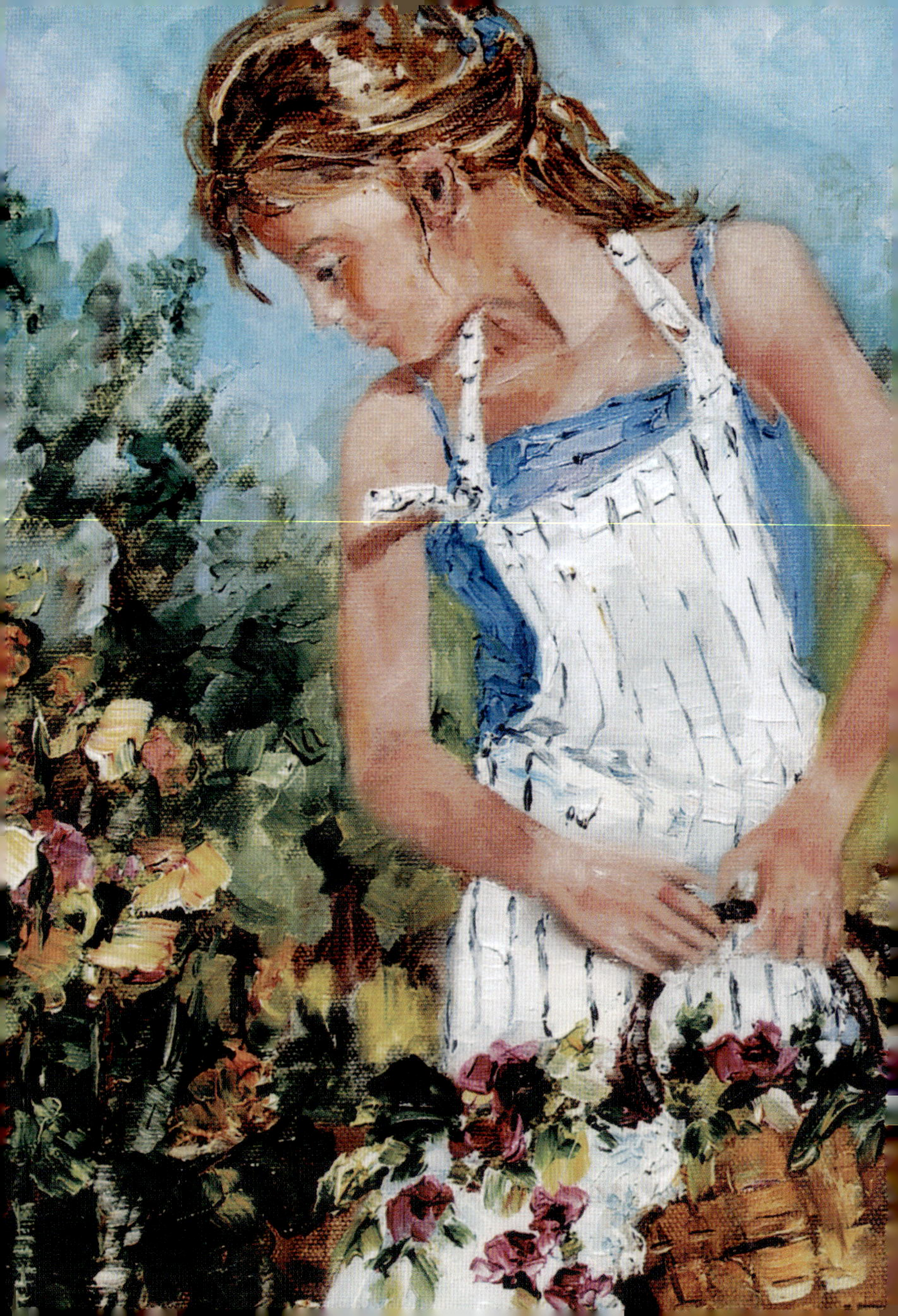

God Is...
MY PROTECTOR

Our home is a place where we feel secure. But high fences and thick walls cannot shield us from tragedy and heartache.

We live in a world that is filled with evil. Sometimes we bring evil upon ourselves by our own actions, but there are also evil forces that we cannot see. In the Bible the book of Job reveals how Satan, the devil, wanted to attack Job, but was not able to because God had put a divine hedge of protection around him and his family. God agreed to lift the protection for a period of time so Job could be tested.

From this account, we get a glimpse into how the evil forces operate in the spiritual realm. Any attempt that they make to interfere in our lives is completely within God's oversight. He watches over us and protects us night and day. When we enter a difficult circumstance, He is always there with us. And if we stay close to Him and seek His guidance, He will help us to steer away from harm.

Loving Father...

Thank you for all the times you have protected me...some, I am sure, that I know nothing about! Help me to become more dependent on you to guide me in my decision-making. Keep me away from evil influences. Give me the courage to avoid places and people that could harm me. I put my trust in you and in your protection. AMEN.

Words to Live By

"Have you not put a hedge around him and his household and everything he has?" Job 1:10

"The angel of the Lord encamps around those who fear Him, and He delivers them." Psalm 34:7

"The Lord is my rock and my fortress and my deliverer; the God of my strength, in whom I will trust; my shield and the horn of my salvation, my stronghold and my refuge; my Savior, you save me from violence." 2 Samuel 22:2 & 3

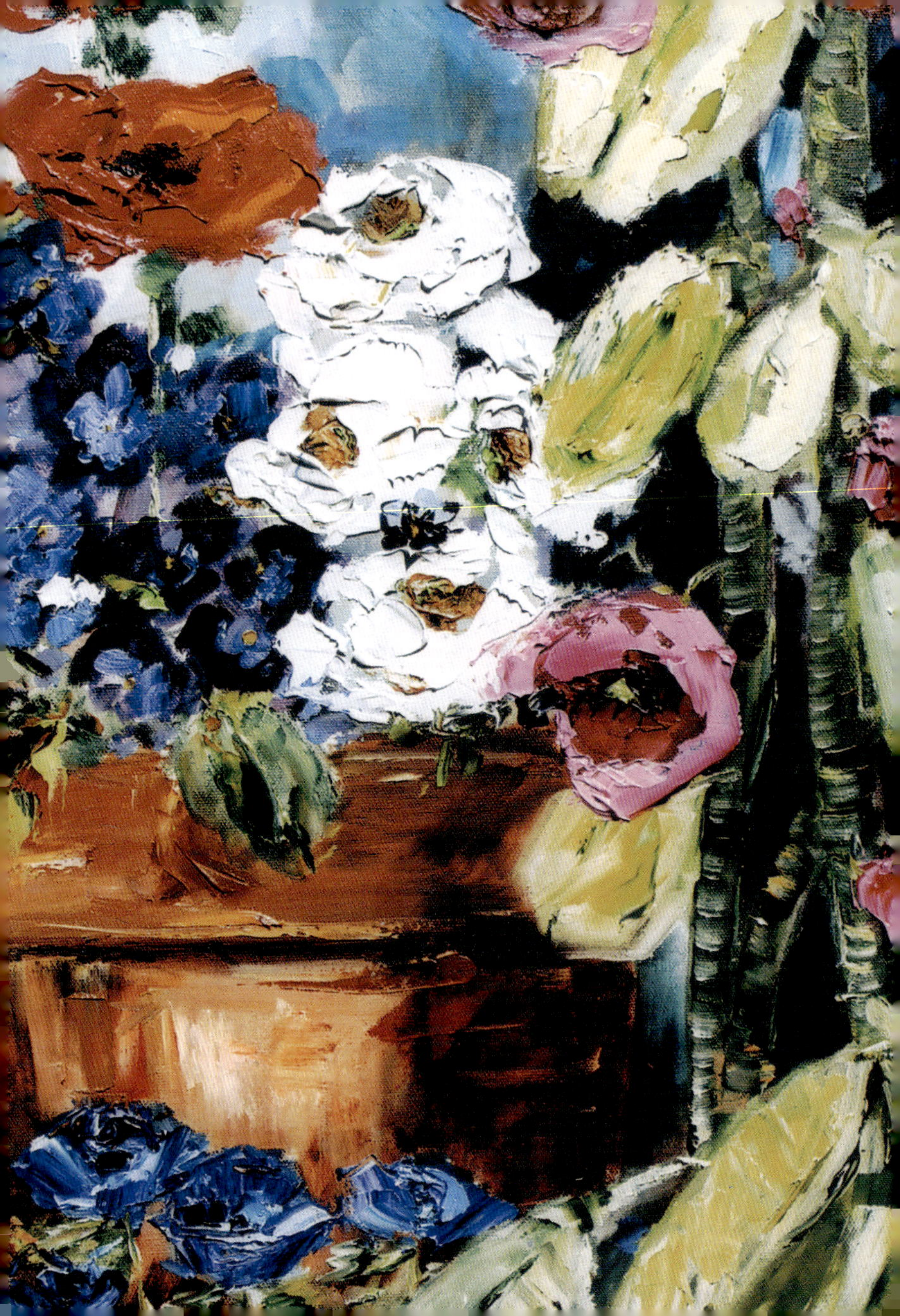

God Is...
MY PROVIDER

We pray each day to ask God to provide our daily needs, and He will honor those prayers. He provides food and shelter, friends and family, a place to live and a place to worship. He sustains and provides for all life on our planet.

But God has also provided for human beings on a much deeper level. He made us spiritual beings as well as physical beings, and He has put within you and me a "God-shaped vacuum" that only He can fill. We may try to overcome the emptiness inside with many different things, but it won't work. God has created us to feel incomplete without Him in our life. Just believing that God exists, and praying occasionally will not fill the vacuum. Why has He done this? Because God wants us in His family.... He desires the closeness and intimacy that one would share with a loving father.

Faithful Father...

Thank you for providing for my material needs. Please give me the wisdom to understand the depth of your love for me. Help me to fill my God-shaped vacuum by setting aside time to spend with you each day. AMEN.

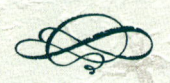

Words to Live By

"As a deer pants for the water brooks, so pants my soul for you, O God." Psalm 42:1

"For God so loved the world that He gave His only begotten Son, that whoever believes in Him should not perish but have everlasting life." John 3:16

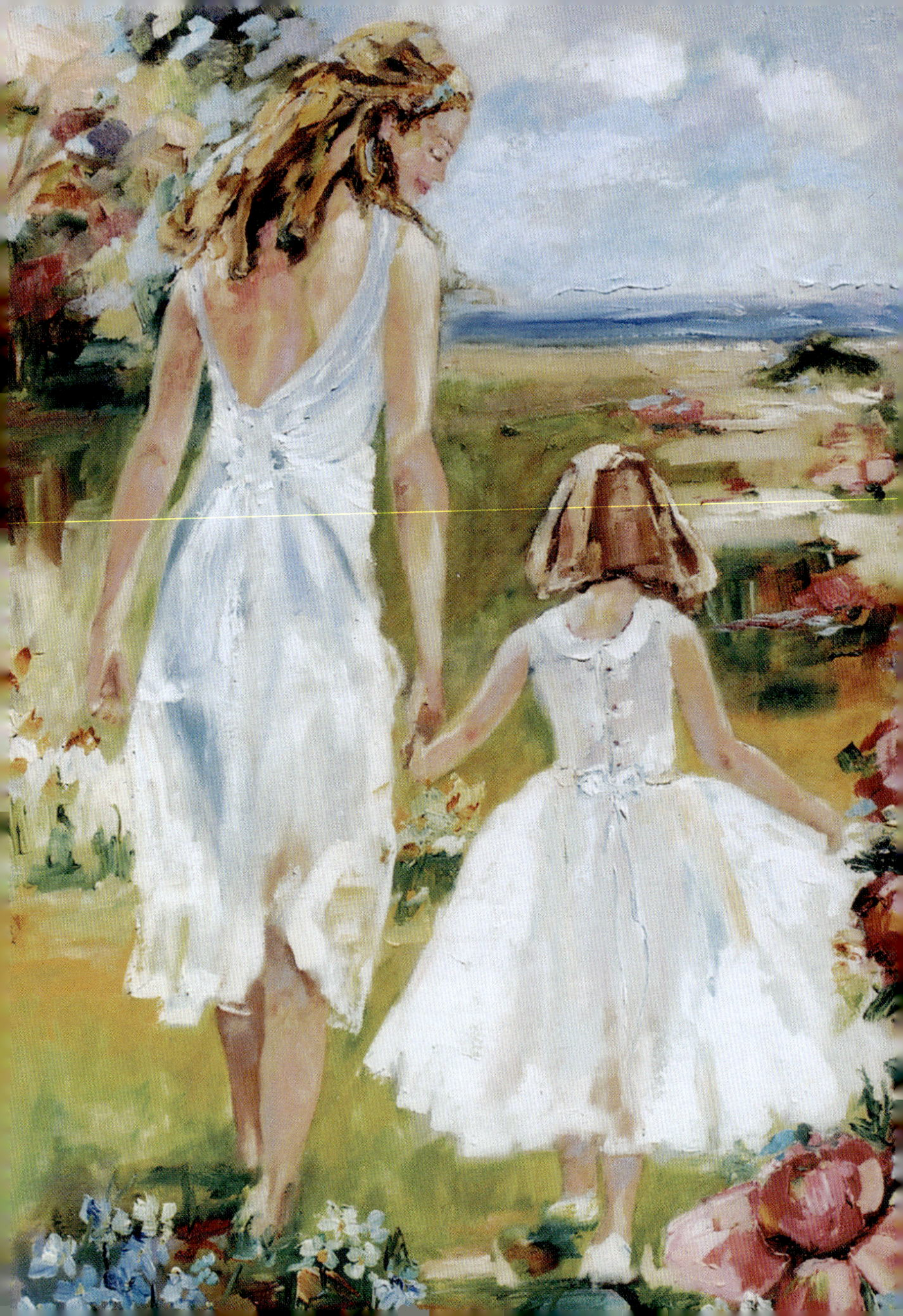

God Is...
MY GUIDE

    Children enjoy walking with a parent, holding their hand. They do not worry about where they are going or what might happen to them. They feel secure and safe, knowing they are being guided and protected by someone they trust.

    God wants us to feel that way about Him. He longs to be our guide through the journey of life. He asks only that you and I trust Him with all our heart. He promises to be with us in good times and bad, to give us encouragement and hope. He will give us guidance when we ask Him for it, and help us to make right choices. If we can put our trust in Him, we will walk down the road of life without fear of the future, secure in the knowledge that He is with us always.

Gracious Father...

Please help me to learn to trust you completely. I want you to guide my life. Give me the peace of mind that comes with putting my confidence in you…no matter what happens. AMEN.

Words to Live By

"Trust in the Lord with all your heart,
And lean not on your own understanding;
In all your ways acknowledge Him,
And He shall direct your paths."
Proverbs 3:5 & 6

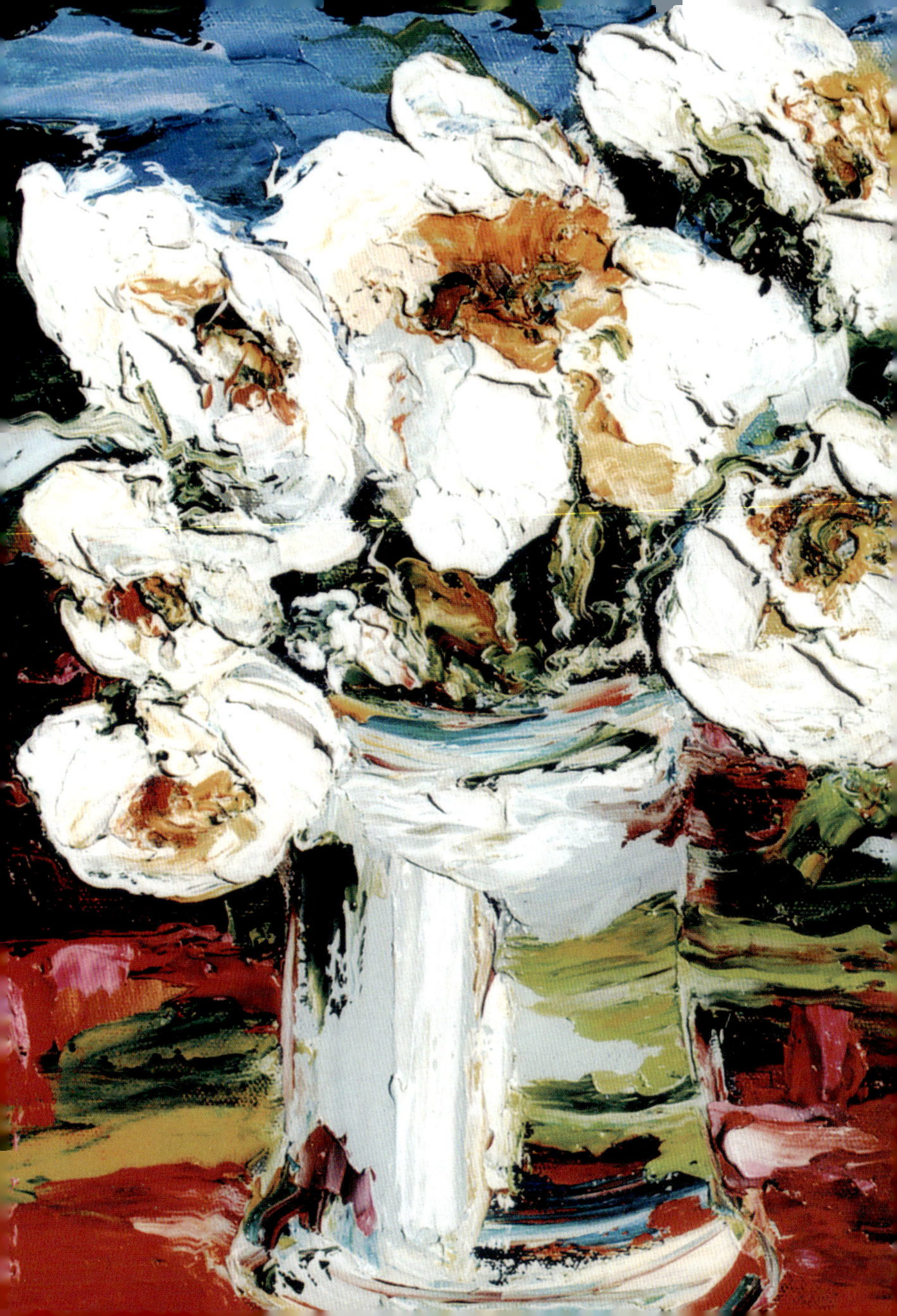

God Is...
FAITHFUL

Nighttime can be scary. Sometimes we recheck locks or leave lights on or play music. Fear of the unknown can be overwhelming. But fear is the opposite of faith. We cannot exercise fear and faith at the same time. God promises that if we put our faith in Him, we need not fear anything. He tells us not to fear because He will strengthen us, help us and uphold us. But do we have the faith to trust Him?

The most important thing about faith is making sure the object of our faith is worthy of our confidence. It would not be wise to put faith in something or someone that has not proven worthy of being trusted. Over and over the Scriptures reveal the faithfulness of God to those who trust Him. We are told that God cannot lie and therefore must keep His promises. Faith based on a promise of God is one built on solid ground!

Loving Father...

I tend to show such little faith. Sometimes I have trouble sleeping because I am fearful. You have been faithful to me but I am not faithful to you. Help me to trust in your promises, because I know when I exercise faith in you, it brings you glory. AMEN.

Words to Live By

"Do not be afraid of sudden terror...for the Lord will be your confidence." Proverbs 3:25 & 26

"Fear not, for I am with you; be not dismayed, for I am your God. I will strengthen you, Yes, I will help you, I will uphold you with My righteous right hand." Isaiah 41:10

"Without faith it is impossible to please Him, for he who comes to God must believe that He is, and that He is a rewarder of those who diligently seek Him." Hebrews 11:6

About the Author

Pamela Gough Bahash serves as a hospital chaplain and teaches women's Bible studies on a regular basis. She came to know God at the age of 25 when someone sowed a seed of faith in her heart and showed her that she could have a relationship with Him.

In her journey she has encountered many challenges, including the tragic death of her oldest son at age ten and the death of her first husband from cancer. The one thing that sustained her through the years is her relationship with God. She has focused on getting to know Him better by discovering His character.

About the Illustrator

January Jorgenson pursued an art career at the University of Northern Iowa, New Mexico State University, Scottsdale Community College and Scottsdale Artist School, where she studied with professional artists.

January paints full time, supplying galleries with her artwork as well as producing commissioned portraits, still lifes, and illustrations for clients. Her paintings are done in oil on canvas and applied with a generous brush stroke and palette knife technique. *Southwest Art Magazine* has identified January as the "artist to start your collection with."

THE LORD IS THE STRENGTH
OF HIS PEOPLE

A FORTRESS OF SALVATION FOR
HIS ANOINTED ONE

SAVE YOUR PEOPLE AND BLESS
YOUR INHERITANCE

BE THEIR SHEPHERD AND CARRY
THEM FOREVER.

Ps.28v8